The Zoo's Who's Who

Lions

Katie Franks

PowerKiDS
press.

New York

Published in 2015 by The Rosen Publishing Group, Inc.
29 East 21st Street, New York, NY 10010

First Edition

Editor: Jennifer Way
Photo Research: Katie Stryker
Book Design: Joe Carney

Photo Credits: Cover Ricardo Reitmeyer/Shutterstock.com; p. 5 ravl/Shutterstock.com; p. 6 Maggy Meyer/Shutterstock.com; pp. 9, 10, 14 iStock/Thinkstock; p. 13 EastVillage Images/Shutterstock.com; p. 17 Michael Fairchild/Photolibrary/Getty Images; p. 18 Jupiterimages/Photos.com/Thinkstock; p. 21 Chris Humphries/Shutterstock.com; p. 22 KA Photography KEVM111/Shutterstock.com.

Library of Congress Cataloging-in-Publication Data

Franks, Katie, author.
 Lions / by Katie Franks. — First edition.
    pages cm. — (The zoo's who's who)
 Includes index.
 ISBN 978-1-4777-6475-6 (library binding) — ISBN 978-1-4777-6564-7 (pbk.) — ISBN 978-1-4777-6565-4 (6-pack)
 1. Lion—Juvenile literature. 2. Zoo animals—Juvenile literature. I. Title.
 QL737.C23F743 2015
 599.757—dc23
                                    2013044968

Manufactured in the United States of America

CPSIA Compliance Information: Batch #WS14PK4: For Further Information contact Rosen Publishing, New York, New York at 1-800-237-9932

Contents

Lions are part of a group called the big cats. Big cats are the only animals in the cat family that roar.

Most wild lions live in Africa.
A small number live in India's
Gir Forest.

Lions live in **grasslands**.
Grasslands are warm and dry.

Adult male lions have **manes**. This makes it easy to tell males from females.

Lions are the only big cats that live in groups. A **pride** is a group of lions.

Wildebeests are one of the animals that lions hunt.

Hyenas are enemies of lions. That is because they hunt the same animals.

17

Lions use their rough tongues to **groom** themselves. They also groom other lions in the pride.

Lions rub heads as a friendly greeting. They do this with the lions in their pride.

Lions are active for a few hours at a time. They may rest up to 20 hours each day!

WORDS TO KNOW

grasslands   groom   manes   pride

WEBSITES

Due to the changing nature of Internet links, PowerKids Press has developed an online list of websites related to the subject of this book. This site is updated regularly. Please use this link to access the list:
www.powerkidslinks.com/zww/lion/

INDEX